God's Secret Agents: Bible Codes to Break

by Catherine Duerr

Cover artwork by Dennis Jones

CPH
SAINT LOUIS

To Mark

R OLEV BLF

__ __ __ __ __ __ __ __

Published by Concordia Publishing House
3558 S. Jefferson Avenue, St. Louis, MO 63118-3968
Manufactured in the United States of America

1 2 3 4 5 6 7 8 9 10 11 10 09 08 07 06 05 04 03 02

Contents

Dear Teacher,

Undoubtedly, the children with whom you work are intrigued with "intrigue." They are fascinated with the complexities of solving a mystery and revel in the feeling of mastery and accomplishment. The activities in this book are designed to draw upon this fascination as a means to engage children in discovering God's truths as made clear to us in His Word.

Invite your children to become secret agents on a mission. The mission you will undertake together is to learn more about living as God's children, loved and redeemed, so your joy in the Lord might be complete and others might come to know more about God's love for us as demonstrated through His Son, Jesus Christ.

Use these reproducible activities together as a unit, or use them individually to expand your Bible teaching. Engage the children in investigation as they delve into God's Word. Encourage them to memorize Scripture verses. Use the verses as a springboard for discussion so they might seek to unlock more of God's riches revealed to us in His Word.

Happy decoding. And may God bless you!

Signed,
The Cryptographer

P.S. For help, check out John 15:12

A Different View

God has important work for you to do, and He has left a message for you in His Word. To get a clearer vision of God's message for you, hold this verse in front of a mirror and then read it aloud.

Trust in the LORD

with all your

heart and lean

not on your own

understanding.

Proverbs 3:5

Your job as one of God's Secret Agents is to discover how He wants us to live as His children. And your source for information to complete this very important mission is the true Word of God—the Bible.

A New Perspective

God's Word is filled with important messages for you as one of His Secret Agents. To get a clearer vision of one of these messages, hold this page in front of a mirror and then read it aloud.

"For My thoughts
are not your
thoughts neither
are your ways My
ways," declares
the LORD.
Isaiah 55:8

As you go about living the Lord's way, remember that He is always there to lead and guide you. Don't trust yourself—seek God's direction in His Word.

A Fresh Look

Sometimes we don't completely understand every message in God's Word. To help you understand why, hold this verse in front of a mirror and then read it aloud.

Now we see but a
poor reflection as in
a mirror; then we
shall see face to
face. Now I know in
part; then I shall
know fully, even as I
am fully known.
1 Corinthians 13:12

As a Secret Agent in God's special mission, you can trust that things you may not understand today will be clear when you get to heaven. Live by faith! Serve the Lord with joy!

Facing Danger

The code below uses pictures instead of letters to spell words. Match the pictures in the message to the letters in the code. Write each letter on the line provided. You will discover a message from God's Word to help you face tricky and dangerous situations.

A =
B =
C =
D =
E =
F =
G =
H =
I =
J =
K =
L =
M =
N =
O =
P =
Q =
R =
S =
T =
U =
V =
W =
X =
Y =
Z =

86:7

God is always with us. When you find yourself facing danger, check out Psalm 121:1–2 and Psalm 23:4.

Facing Problems

Who is there for you when you need help the most? Break this code to find out. Match each picture in the message with the coordinating letter in the code. Then write the letter in the space provided.

A =
B =
C =
D =
E =
F =
G =
H =
I =
J =
K =
L =
M =
N =
O =
P =
Q =
R =
S =
T =
U =
V =
W =
X =
Y =
Z =

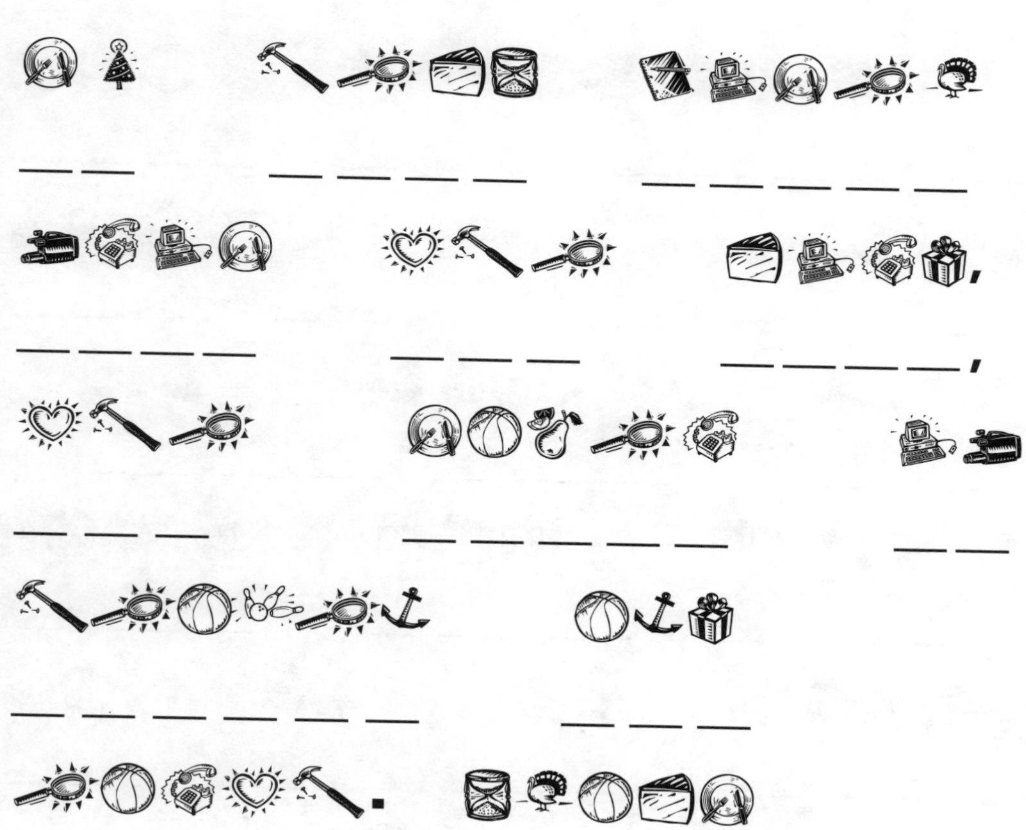

___ ___ ___ ___ ___ ___ ___ ___ ___ . ___ ___ ___ ___ ___ **121:2**

Is there a problem you are facing? Do you need help? Check out Psalm 86:7 to see why you can turn to God for help.

Facing Fears

Who helps you through really scary times? The picture code below tells who. Match each picture in the secret message with a letter in the code. Write the letter in the space provided to spell out the message. And trust in the One who gives you peace.

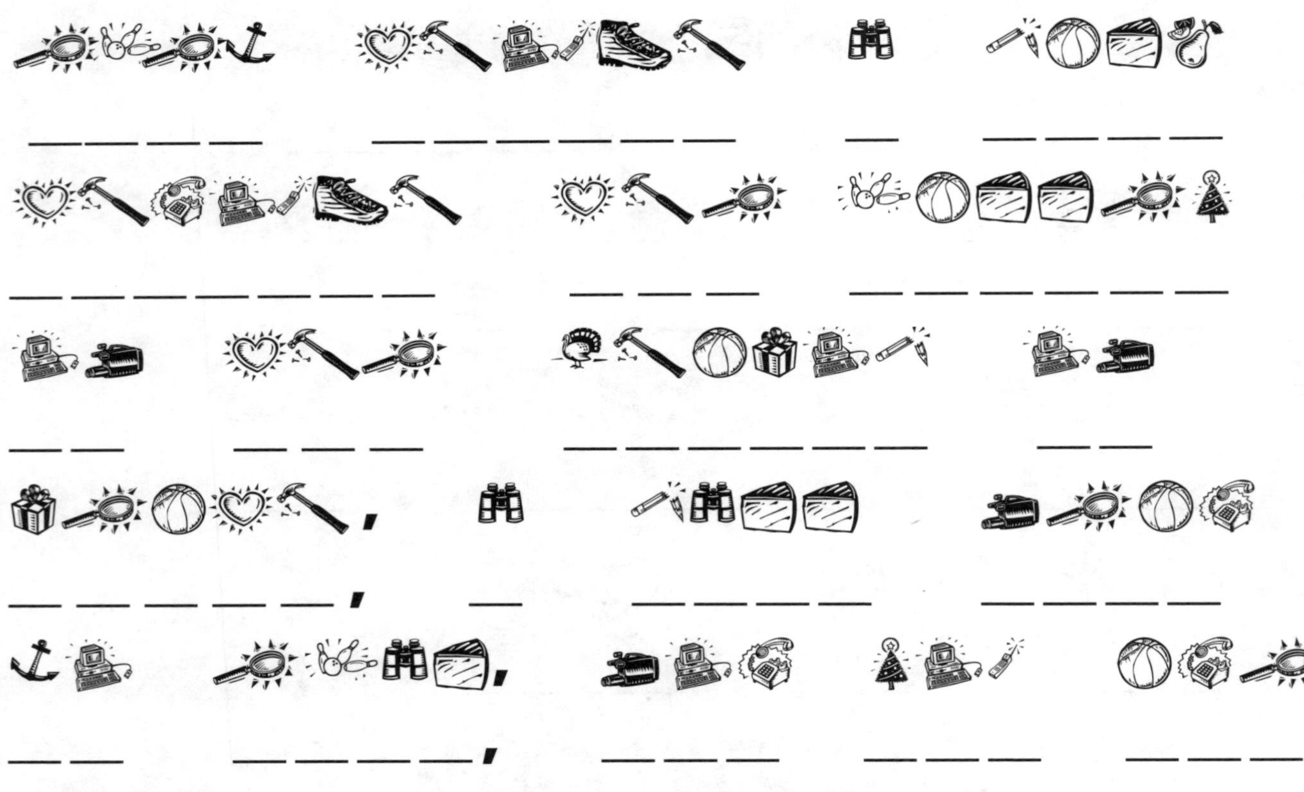

23:4

Wherever you go, whatever you do, God is right beside you. Read Psalm 46:1 for evidence.

Facing Danger

Sometimes it may seem as if you are all alone—but you're not! Break the following code to discover who is always by your side. Match the pictures in the puzzle with the letters in the code. Write the letters in the spaces provided.

A =
B =
C =
D =
E =
F =
G =
H =
I =
J =
K =
L =
M =
N =
O =
P =
Q =
R =
S =
T =
U =
V =
W =
X =
Y =
Z =

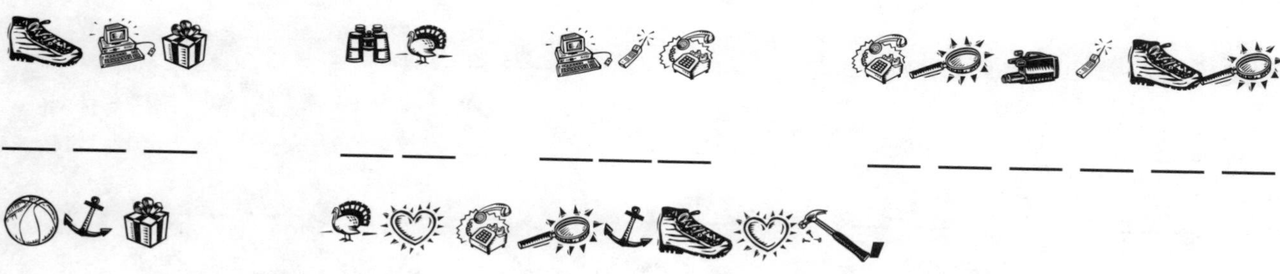

__ __ __   __ __   __ __ __   __ __ __ __ __ __

__ __ __   __ __ __ __ __ __ __ __ __ ,

__ __   __ __ __ __ - __ __ __ __ __ __ __

__ __ __ __   __ __   __ __ __ __ __ __ __ __ .

__ __ __ __ __ __ **46:1**

Whenever you feel afraid or lonely, remember that God is your source of strength. Trust in Him to provide for your every need.

Constant Protection

Use the code below to match pictures with letters. Write each letter in the space provided. Then spell out the secret message to discover what protection you always have against things that may cause you harm.

A =
B =
C =
D =
E =
F =
G =
H =
I =
J =
K =
L =
M =
N =
O =
P =
Q =
R =
S =
T =
U =
V =
W =
X =
Y =
Z =

6:11

As one of God's Secret Agents, you are always protected. You cannot defend yourself against the devil. But God sent His Son, Jesus, to defeat the devil for you. Trust in His power, strength, and protection.

God's Armor

As a Secret Agent you need protection. God has provided His armor for your use. What is God's armor? Crack the code to find out. The first letter of the alphabet is matched to 01. The last letter of the alphabet is matched to 26. Fill in the numbers in between. To solve the puzzle, match the numbers in the clue to the letters in the code.

A	B	C	D	E	F	G	H	I	J	K	L	M
01												

N	O	P	Q	R	S	T	U	V	W	X	Y	Z
												26

19 20 01 14 04 06 09 18 13 20 08 05 14,
__ __ __ __ __ __ __ __ __ __ __ __ __,

23 09 20 08 20 08 05 02 05 12 20 15 06
__ __ __ __ __ __ __ __ __ __ __ __ __

20 18 21 20 08 02 21 03 11 12 05 04
__ __ __ __ __ __ __ __ __ __ __ __

01 18 15 21 14 04 25 15 21 18 23 01 09 19 20,
__ __ __ __ __ __ __ __ __ __ __ __ __ __ __,

23 09 20 08 20 08 05
__ __ __ __ __ __ __

02 18 05 01 19 20 16 12 01 20 05 15 06
__ __ __ __ __ __ __ __ __ __ __ __ __

18 09 07 08 20 05 15 21 19 14 05 19 19 09 14
__ __ __ __ __ __ __ __ __ __ __ __ __ __ __

16 12 01 03 05.
__ __ __ __ __. Ephesians 6:14

It isn't made of steel or iron, but God's armor is stronger than anything and everything. Read Ephesians 6:10 and remember that He is the source of the greatest power and strength.

*

Surrounded

Something special happens inside when you know you can trust God and His armor. What is it? This code gives you an important clue. The first letter of the alphabet is matched to 01. The last letter matches 26. Fill in the numbers in between. To solve the puzzle, match the numbers in the clue to the letters in the code.

A	B	C	D	E	F	G	H	I	J	K	L	M
01												

N	O	P	Q	R	S	T	U	V	W	X	Y	Z
												26

02 21 20 12 05 20 01 12 12 23 08 15 20 01 11 05

___ ___ ___ ___ ___ ___ ___ ___ ___ ___ ___ ___ ___ ___ ___ ___

18 05 06 21 07 05 09 14 25 15 21 02 05

___ ___ ___ ___ ___ ___ ___ ___ ___ ___ ___ ___ ___

07 12 01 04 ; 12 05 20 20 08 05 13 05 22 05 18

___ ___ ___ ___; ___ ___ ___ ___ ___ ___ ___ ___ ___ ___ ___

19 09 14 07 06 15 18 10 15 25 ... 20 08 15 19 05

___ ___ ___ ___ ___ ___ ___ ___ ___ ___... ___ ___ ___ ___ ___

23 08 15 12 15 22 05 25 15 21 18 14 01 13 05

___ ___ ___ ___ ___ ___ ___ ___ ___ ___ ___ ___ ___ ___ ___

13 01 25 18 05 10 15 09 03 05 09 14 25 15 21.

___ ___ ___ ___ ___ ___ ___ ___ ___ ___ ___ ___ ___ ___ ___.

Psalm 5:11

Rejoice in God's love. Find comfort in His strength. Read Psalm 5:12 and put your full trust in God as He surrounds you with the shield of His love.

Rescue

The puzzle below helps you discover more about how God protects His Secret Agents. The first letter of the alphabet is matched to 01. The last letter matches 26. Fill in the numbers in between. To solve the puzzle, match the numbers in the clue to the letters in the code.

A	B	C	D	E	F	G	H	I	J	K	L	M
01												

N	O	P	Q	R	S	T	U	V	W	X	Y	Z
												26

06 15 18   08 05   23 09 12 12   03 15 13 13 01 14 04

__ __ __   __ __   __ __ __ __   __ __ __ __ __ __ __

08 09 19   01 14 07 05 12 19

__ __ __   __ __ __ __ __ __

03 15 14 03 05 18 14 09 14 07   25 15 21   20 15

__ __ __ __ __ __ __ __ __ __   __ __ __   __ __

07 21 01 18 04   25 15 21   09 14

__ __ __ __ __   __ __ __   __ __

01 12 12   25 15 21 18   23 01 25 19 .

__ __ __   __ __ __ __   __ __ __ __.   Psalm 91:11

Can you name a time of trouble when you turned to God? Turn to Psalm 91:14–16 in your Bible to read more about God's promise to rescue you.

The Solution to the Problem

To decode this message, first solve the math problem. Then use the decoder below to match the answer to the math problem to the letter in the code. When you have decoded this message, it will tell you how to solve other problems. **Hint:** 39÷3=13=M.

A	B	C	D	E	F	G	H	I	J	K	L	M
01	02	03	04	05	06	07	08	09	10	11	12	13
N	**O**	**P**	**Q**	**R**	**S**	**T**	**U**	**V**	**W**	**X**	**Y**	**Z**
14	15	16	17	18	19	20	21	22	23	24	25	26

39÷3 12+13 72÷9 83-78 3X4 64÷4 24÷8 8+7 25-12 2+3 11+8 2+4

____

3X6 9+6 8+5 10+10 3+5 18-13 4+8 3X5 29-11 3+1, 13+7 17-9

____

1X5 20-7 29-28 5+6 12-7 9+9 8+7 11-5 2X4 17-12 1+0 19+3

____

18-13 2X7 6-5 8+6 2+2 14-9 13-12 13+5 12+8 6+2 .

________________________________ **PSALM 121:2**

2X5 25÷5 12+7 3X7 25-6 6÷6 2X7 15+4 48-25 2+3 3X6 100÷20

____

2+2, "3X3 39-38 39÷3 4X5 2X4 49-44 13+10 1X1 14+11 94-93 18-

____

4 26-22 2X10 64÷8 33-28 100÷5 9X2 84÷4 89-69 72÷9 100-99 12+2

____

96÷24 40÷2 48÷6 45÷9 3X4 3X3 3X2 3+2. 28÷2 3X5 45÷3 18-4

____

87-82 18÷6 79-64 74-61 60÷12 12+7 17+3 3X5 97-77 88÷11 30÷6

____

42÷7 1953-1952 27-7 16÷2 45÷9 36÷2 80÷16 4X6 9÷3 22-17 2X8

____

12+8 2X10 96÷12 2X9 8+7 3X7 56÷8 24÷3 52-39 1+4 ."

________________________________ **JOHN 14:6**

Turn to God in prayer. He has the solution to every problem we face!

Communication Key

A Secret Agent must be a good communicator. And two things that are vital to good communication are listening and hearing. Here is a code that hearing-impaired people use to listen to one another. Use the sign language code to "hear" these important messages.

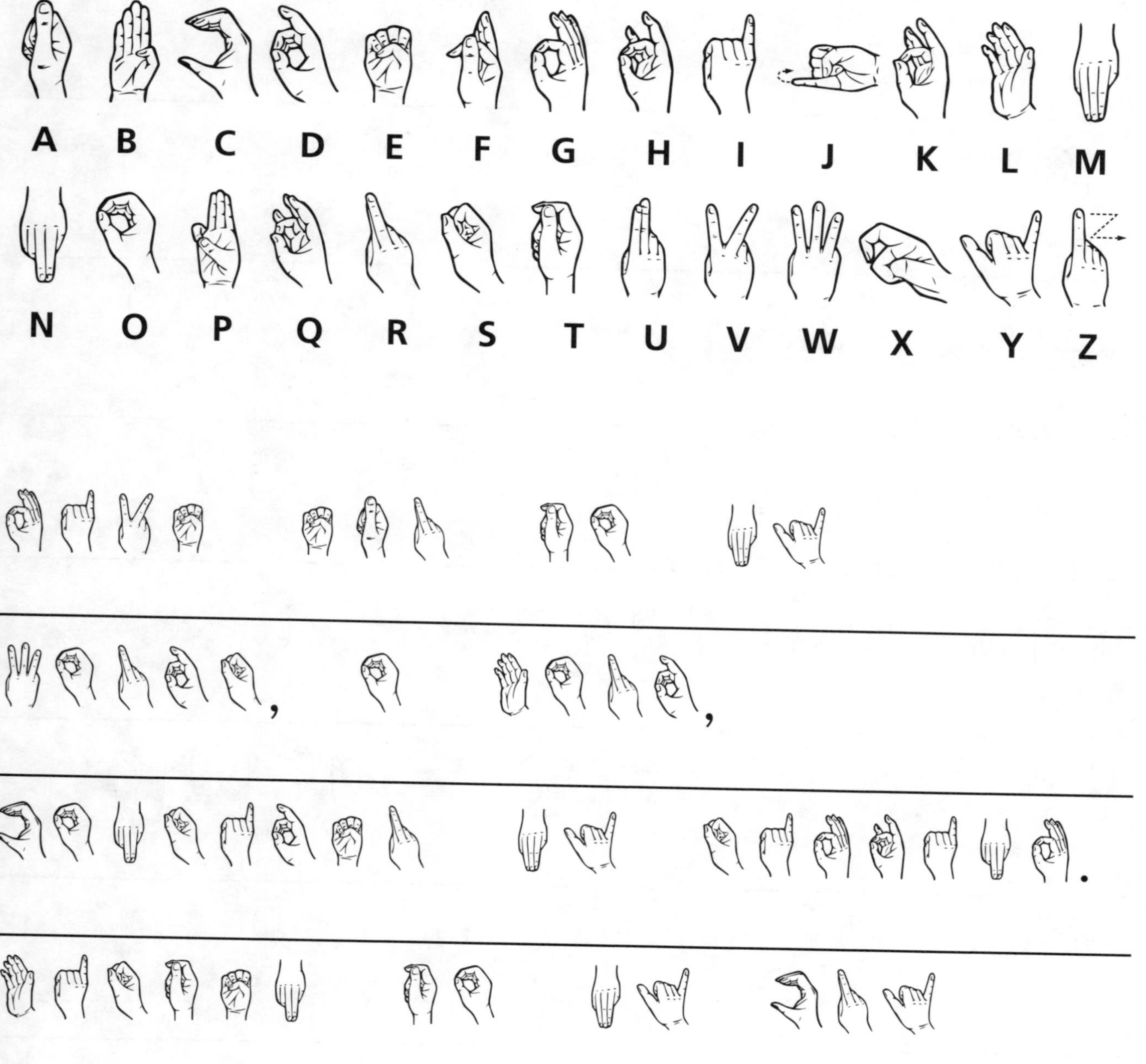

Puzzle continues on pages 18 and 19.

PSALM 5:1–3

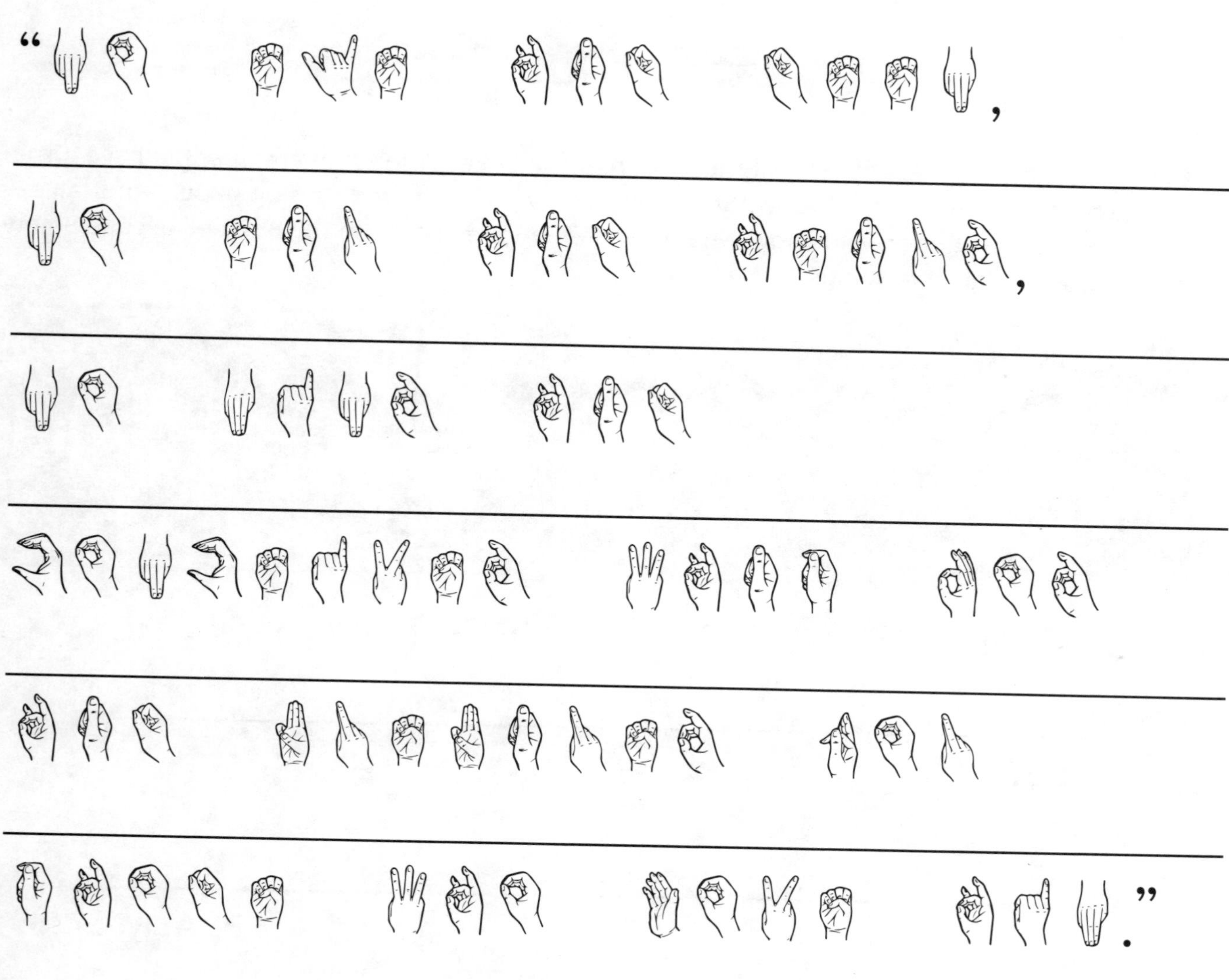

1 CORINTHIANS 2:9

God's goodness and faithfulness are fantastic! Share this fantastic message with everyone! Try signing a Bible verse to a friend. Use one of these verses or sign one of your favorites.

What Do You See?

A good Secret Agent uses all the resources available. Vision-impaired people have a special code that allows them to read with their fingers. By feeling raised dots on paper—or Braille—they read with their fingers and know what is written on the page. Use the Braille-like code below to find out what valuable things you can to see.

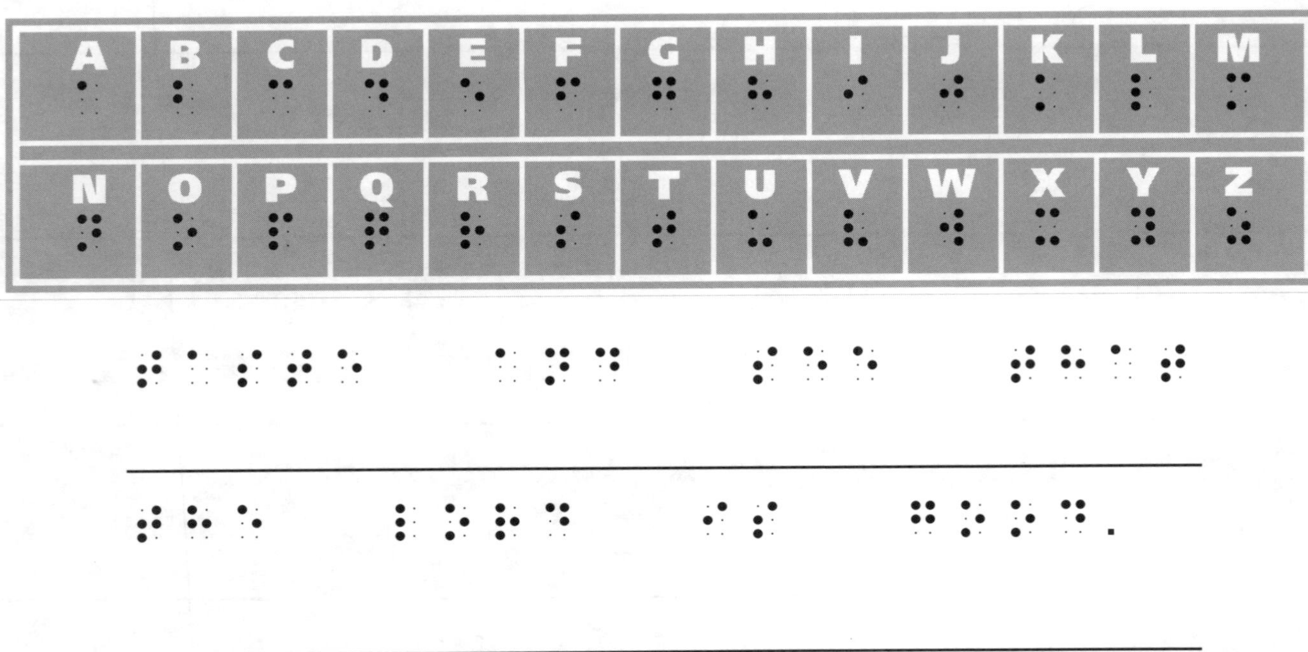

PSALM 34:8

God gives us a lot to see. Use the Braille code to decode this message and see how great He is.

PSALM 66:5

These messages give vital information about what we see. Decode them with the Braille code.

PSALM 119:18

JOHN 3:3

MATTHEW 5:8

Make a list of all the things God helps you see that give a glimpse of His love.

You Are Lost!

Pretend that you are on a super secret mission—but you are lost and you know you can't find your way on your own. You discover a hidden message; however, all the letters of the message are rearranged. Write the first letter from the first row on the blank line below. Then write the first letter from the second row next to it. Next, write the second letter from the first row beside that. Keep going until you have correctly arranged all the letters. (The first few letters have been done for you.) The last step is to draw a line between the words where spaces should be.

____

____.

JOEL 2:32

God gives His Secret Agents many messages of comfort in His Word. This verse helps us remember that we can be certain of a safe mission in His care.

Three-Part Message

This three-part message holds very important information for you. All the letters in the message are rearranged. To break the code, write the first letter from the first row on the blank line below. Then write the first letter from the second row next to it. Third, write the second letter from the first row next to that. Keep going until you have correctly arranged all the letters. The last step is to draw a line between the words where spaces should be.

A D H S S H T E R M S D S V N T R A L F
N T I I W A H P O I E U E E E E N L I E

____

______________________________ . **1 JOHN 2:25**

F R T S Y R C Y U A E E N A E T R U H A T A D H S O F O
O I I B G A E O H V B E S V D H O G F I H N T I N T R M

____

_____________________________________ ...

Y U S L E I I T E I T F O N T Y O K S T A N O E A B A T
O R E V S T S H G F O G D O B W R S O H T O N C N O S

____

____

____________________________ . **EPHESIANS 2:8–9**

Is there anything you can do to save yourself? Jesus died on the cross and rose again for the forgiveness of sin. Only through Jesus can you have the promise of eternal life. Memorize 1 John 5:11 and share this Good News with others.

Stay on Track

Wherever we go, whatever we do, it is important to always have one important focus. What is it? Moses and the Israelites give us a clue. In the code below, the spaces between words have been moved. Instead of spaces in the correct places, there is a space after every five letters. Divide the string of letters into words, write the words on the line provided, then read the message. **Hint:** The first word is THE, which leaves LO to go with RD in the next group of letters, forming LORD.

THELO RDISM YSTRE NGTHA NDMYS ONGHE HASBE COMEM YSALV ATION HEISM YGODA NDIWI LLPRA ISEHI MMYFA THERS GODAN DIWIL LEXAL THIM

____

____

__________________________________ . **EXODUS 15:2**

Moses and the Israelites had a difficult journey, but they stayed focused on God. When you are faced with difficulties, remember this story and look to God to help you stay on track. Look in the Bible for these reminders: Romans 10:13 and John 3:16.

Twice the Fun

This important message is tricky because it is hidden in two codes. To break the code and discover the message, you must first reverse the order of each group of five letters. For example, the first group—OGROF—should be transposed to FORGO.

OGROF OLOSD HTDEV LROWE TAHTD VAGEH OSIHE DNAEN SYLNO AHTNO EOHWT EBREV EVEIL IHNIS LAHSM PTONL HSIRE AHTUB ETEEV LLANR EFI

____

____

____

Now that you have reversed all the letters in the groups, find the hidden message by rearranging the spaces between the words. The first word is FOR.

____

____

____________________________________ . **JOHN 3:16**

God's message of salvation through Jesus Christ is for all people. As God's Secret Agent, you can share this Good News. Read more about it in 1 John 2:25 and Mark 8:35.

*

Tricky Triple Teaser

Decoding this hidden message requires your full attention. First, draw a line after every five letters in the code. Then reverse the order of the five letters and write them on the line below. The first letter on the line should be F.

H W R O F R E V E O S T N A W V A S O T L S I H E I W
E F I S O L L L U B T I E E O H W T O L R E V I H S E
S E F I L S E M R O F O F D N A G E H T R L E P S O S
L L I W T I E V A

____

____

____

Now you're ready to read the message. Divide the words by putting word spaces in the right places, and write the message on the lines below.

____

____

______________________________________ . **MARK 8:35**

Congratulations, Secret Agent! You have decoded a very important message the whole world needs to know. For further guidance, read Romans 10:13.

Cooking Diamonds?

Imagine that a man wearing a trench coat and a hat pulled down low stands close behind you and says, "A carpenter went out to cook his diamonds." What does that mean? Nothing, unless you know the code. Below are the code words and what they represent. When you look at the list, you will find that "carpenter" actually means "farmer," but the sentence still doesn't make sense. To reveal the mysterious message, replace all the underscored words with encoded words.

diamonds	seed
mountain	plant
sea	soil
hammer	crop
cook	sow
lizard	bird
purple	rocky
king	sun
swallowed	choked
carpenter	farmer
brave	quick
pudding	root
flower	thorn
danced	fell
spoke	sprang
frogs	ears

"A <u>carpenter</u> went out to <u>cook</u> his <u>diamonds</u>.

____

As he was scattering the <u>diamonds</u>, some <u>danced</u>

____

along the path, and the <u>lizards</u> came and ate it up.

____

Some <u>danced</u> on <u>purple</u> places, where it did not have

____

much <u>sea</u>. It <u>spoke</u> up <u>bravely</u>, because the <u>sea</u> was

____

shallow. But when the <u>king</u> came up,

____

the <u>mountains</u> were scorched, and they withered

____

because they had no <u>pudding</u>. Other <u>diamonds</u>

____

<u>danced</u> among <u>flowers</u>, which grew up and <u>swallowed</u> the <u>mountains</u>. Still other

____

<u>diamonds</u> <u>danced</u> on good <u>sea</u>, where it produced a <u>hammer</u>—a hundred, sixty or

____

thirty times what was <u>cooked</u>. He who has <u>frogs</u>, let him hear." Matthew 13:3–9

____

Read Matthew 13:18–23 in your Bible for clues to the meaning of this message. Check verse 19 to see which diamonds are being cooked.

Crossed Codes

This looks like a crossword puzzle that someone has been working on and hasn't finished. But if you look closely, the answers aren't necessarily words. There is a code hidden in this puzzle. Start at the top letter and read left to right, working your way down to find the hidden message.

____

____

______________________________________ . PSALM 119:11

God has planted His message in our hearts. He will help you share it with your friends.

Abundant Evidence

"Abundant" means "more than enough." In the Bible, we learn about the abundant evidence of God's love and grace. The following messages have an abundance of letters. Start with the second letter in the code and cross out every other letter. Divide the remaining letters into words and write them on the lines. The Bible messages will be abundantly clear to you!

D ~~T~~ E ~~H~~ L ~~E~~ I L G O H R T D Y W O I U L R L S O E P L E F N I T
N H T E H H E E L A O V R E D N A S N T D H H E E S W T I O
L R L E G H I O V U E S Y E O O U F T H H I E S D B E O
S U I N R T E Y S T O O F S Y E O N U D R R H A E I A N R O T

____

____

________________________________ . **PSALM 37:4**

T N H Y E O L U O R R L D A G N I D V I E N S S S E T A R S E
O N N G A T N H D T T O O H B I L S E P S E S O A P L L L E T T
H H E E W L O O R R K D O B F L Y E O S U S R E H S A H N I D
S S P Y E O O U P W L I E L W L I L T E H N P D E T A O C M E

____

____

________________________________ . **PSALM 29:11**

These verses are evidence of God's abundant blessings. Your mission as God's Secret Agent is to share His abundant love with others—especially the Good News of His love that overflowed when He sent Jesus to be our Savior.

The Evidence Is Abundant

God gives lovingly and abundantly to His Secret Agents. What are some of these blessings? Decode the following messages to find out. Start with the second letter and cross out every other letter. Divide the remaining letters into words and write them on the lines. The Bible messages will be abundantly clear to you!

F M O A R N T Y H N E A L T O I R O D N G S I B V U E T S W W I I L
S L D B O O M R A R N O D W F F R R O O M M H N I O S N M E O
T U H T E H L C O O R M D E W K I N L O L W M L A E K D E
G Y E O A U N T D H U E N H D E E A R D S N T O A T N T D H I E N T G

____

____

______________________________ . **PROVERBS 2:6**

A A N I D L M I Y F G Y O O D U W P I A L Y L A M T E T E E T
N A T L I L O Y N O T U O R T N H E E E C D O S M A M C A C N O D R S
D O I F N T G H T E O L H O I R S D G Y L O O U R R I G O O U D
S T R H I A C T H I E G S I I V N E C Y H O R U I T S H T I J S E D S A U Y S

____

____

______________________________ . **PHILIPPIANS 4:19**

F A O N R D T C H A E R L E O F R U D L G L O Y D F I O S L A L
S O U W N T A H N E D M S Y H O I U E W L I D L T L H A E L L
W O A R Y D S B B E E S A T T O T W H S E F T A O V P O N
R E A V N E D R H A O T N T O H R E N B O O G T O T O O D M T D
H O I N N O G T D T O U E R S N H A E S W I I D T E
H F H R O O L M D A F N R Y O O M F T T H H O E S C E O W M H
M O A S N E D W S A I L G K I I V S E B Y L O A U M T E O L D E A S Y S

____

____

________________________________ . **PSALM 84:11**

There is one more message tucked into these codes. It can be found in the letters you crossed out. Put those letters together, divide them into words and you will discover another message about the abundance of God's love.

The LORD will open the heavens, the stone house of His bounty, to send rain on your land in season and to bless all the work of your hands. You will lend to m____________________________________

____

____________________________ . **DEUTERONOMY 28:12–13**

If you need help with these messages, look up the verses in your Bible. The evidence of God's love is abundantly clear in His Word.

Our Helper

As we pursue our mission, we are not alone. We have a helper. You can have help as you decode these next messages about who your helper is. Cut out the circles on these pages. Put the small one on top of the large one and put a brad through the center of both circles.

Use the decoder to reveal these important messages. The two-letter clue is given at the beginning of each code. The code letters are on the inner circle. The plain alphabet, or the answers, are on the outer circle. Always work from the inside out. The first code says A=D. Rotate the discs until the "A" on the outer circle lines up with the "D" on the inner circle. Once they are lined up, you can decode the first message.

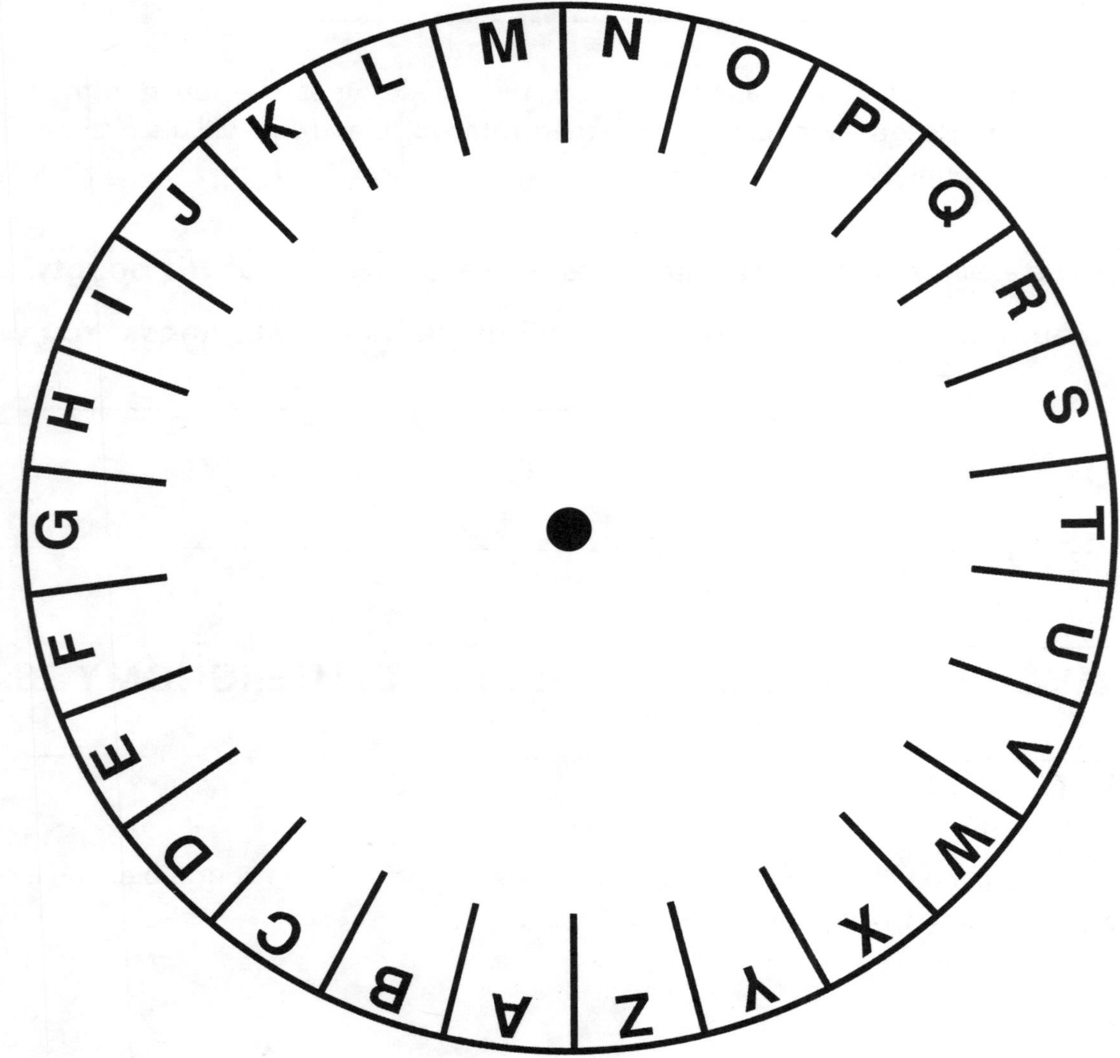

A = D

"PBX ATLROXWTI, PBX BTWG OYNINP, JBTE PBX

CDPBXI JNWW OXRZ NR EG RDEX, JNWW PXDAB

GTL DWW PBNRVO DRZ JNWW IXENRZ GTL TC

XKXIGPBNRV N BDKX ODNZ PT GTL."

JOHN 14:26

A = T

"YNB EAN QJFF COUOJMO ZAQOC QKOS BKO

KAFE VZJCJB UADOV AS EAN."

ACTS 1:8

A = B

DTW FJYGYD FWBGMTWF BOO DTYLRF, WAWL

DTW QWWJ DTYLRF KE RKQ.

1 CORINTHIANS 2:10

A = O

XOU WFJ GVK VH FVBJ HDZZ UVE TDWF OZZ

SVU OCK BJOLJ OQ UVE WMEQW DC FDX, QV

WFOW UVE XOU VRJMHZVT TDWF FVBJ PU WFJ

BVTJM VH WFJ FVZU QBDMDW.

ROMANS 15:13

God's message of salvation is not hidden in a code and you don't need special tools to find it. It's provided for all in His Holy Bible. Share these verses with people who need to hear the Gospel.

Strength and Power

This message reminds you of the source of the strength and power necessary for your mission. To reveal the message, use the shifted alphabet code. Write the first six letters of the encoded message in the space below as shown in the sample.

L FDQ GR HYHUBWKLQJ WKURXJK KLP ZKR JLYHV PH VWUHQJWK.

L	F D Q	G R
M	G E R	H S
N	H F S	I T
O	I G T	J U
P	J H U	K V
Q	K I V	L W
R	L J W	M X
S	M K X	N Y
T	N L Y	O Z
U	O M Z	P A
__	__ __ __	__ __
__	__ __ __	__ __
__	__ __ __	__ __
__	__ __ __	__ __
__	__ __ __	__ __
__	__ __ __	__ __
__	__ __ __	__ __
__	__ __ __	__ __
__	__ __ __	__ __
__	__ __ __	__ __

Next, in the column beneath the letter L, write the rest of the alphabet in order. When you get to Z, continue with A and keep going until you finish with K. Do this with each of the letters at the top of the columns. So, the column under the letter F begins with G, is followed by H, and so on. The column under D begins with E, is followed by F, and continues. A sample is shown for you at the left.

Once you have run through the alphabet under the first six letters in the code, look through the combinations of letters until you find one that spells words. The third line from the bottom spells the words "I CAN DO". Now you know that L stands for I, F stands for C, and so forth.

__	__ __ __	__ __
__	__ __ __	__ __
__	__ __ __	__ __
__	__ __ __	__ __
__	__ __ __	__ __
__	__ __ __	__ __

In the space below, write the letters of the alphabet in order from left to right, the way you would normally see them. Above the I, place an L. Next, above the J write the letter M, above the K write N. Continue through the alphabet from L to K. The top row are the code letters, the bottom row is the alphabet. To crack the code, look at the top row for the letter in the message and match it to the letter below it in the alphabet. Now you have the code and can decipher the message.

_ _ _ _ _ _ _ _ _ **M N** _ _ _ _ _ _ _ _ _ _ _ _ _ _ _

A B C D E F G H I J K L M N O P Q R S T U V W X Y Z

L FDQ GR HYHUBWKLQJ WKURXJK KLP

I CAN DO E____________________

ZKR JLYHV PH VWUHQJWK.

______________________________ . **PHILIPPIANS 4:13**

As one of God's Secret Agents, rely on Him to give you strength for any mission in His name. Read Philippians 4:6 for more.

Hidden Directions

Your mission is to convey important information that can help others learn about God and His love. Important truths are hidden in these codes. Communicating is in the telling. First, you must reconstruct the code. Start at A and write each letter of the alphabet until you have finished. Then, on the line below, write the alphabet backward beginning with Z. Be sure to write the letters so they align with the one above or below it.

A ____

Z ____

To reveal the clues, match the letters on the second line of the code above with the words in the messages below, and write them in the space provided.

BLF SZEV NZWV PMLDM GL NV GSV KZGS

____

LU ORUV; BLF DROO UROO NV DRGS QLB

____

RM BLFI KIVHVMXV, DRGS VGVIMZO

____

KOVZHFIVH ZG BLFI IRTSG SZMW.

______________________________________ PSALM 16:11

WLM'G OVG ZMBLMV OLLP WLDM LM BLF YVXZFHV

____

BLF ZIV BLFMT, YFG HVG ZM VCZNKOV ULI GSV

____

YVORVEVIH RM HKVVXS, RM ORUV, RM OLEV,

____

RM UZRGS ZMW RM KFIRGB.

______________________________________ 1 TIMOTHY 4:12

To double-check the truth of this message, look up these Bible passages: Psalm 32:18, Proverbs 3:6, and Isaiah 45:2. And remember to always look to God as your leader and source of joy.

Secret Source

Secret Agents know where to get the best encouragement to complete their mission. What is your source? To reveal the secret source identified in the message below, use the shifted alphabet code. Write the first five letters of the encoded message as shown in the sample below.

OJ CDH WZ OCZ KJRZM AJM ZQZM VIY ZQZM. VHZI.

O	J		C	D	H
P	K		D	E	I
Q	L		E	F	J
___	___		___	___	___
___	___		___	___	___
___	___		___	___	___
___	___		___	___	___

Next, in a column beneath the letter O, write the rest of the alphabet in order. When you get to Z, continue with A and keep going until you finish with N. Do this with each of the letters you wrote. So, the column under the letter J begins with K, is followed by L, and so on. The column under C begins with D, is followed by E, and continues. A sample is shown for you.

Once you have run through the alphabet under the first five letters in the code, look through the combinations of letters until you find one that spells words. One of the combinations will spell "TO HIM." Now you know that O stands for T, J stands for O, and so forth.

Next, write the letters of the alphabet in order from left to right, the way you would normally see them. Above the T, place an O. Next, above the O write the letter J. Continue through the alphabet. The top row are the code letters, the bottom row is the alphabet. To crack the code, look at the top row for the letter in the message and match it to the letter below it in the alphabet. Now you have the code and can decipher the message.

														J					O						
A	B	C	D	E	F	G	H	I	J	K	L	M	N	**O**	P	Q	R	S	**T**	U	V	W	X	Y	Z

OJ CDH WZ OCZ KJRZM AJM

____

ZQZM VIY ZQZM. VHZI.

_______________________________ **1 PETER 5:11**

Faith in Jesus is your source for everything you need. Believe in Him! Hold on to Him! Say a prayer of thanksgiving!

True Clue

Secret Agents have a source for strength and power that many people do not understand. To reveal the source of this power identified in the message below, use the shifted alphabet code. Write the first six letters of the encoded message as shown in the sample below.

TCF HVS ASGGOUS CT HVS QFCGG WG TCCZWGVBSGG HC HVCGS KVC OFS

T	**C**	**F**	**H**	**V**	**S**
U	D	G	I	W	T
V	E	H	J	X	U
W	F	I	K	Y	V
X	G	J	L	Z	W
Y	H	K	M	A	X
___	___	___	___	___	___
___	___	___	___	___	___
___	___	___	___	___	___
___	___	___	___	___	___
___	___	___	___	___	___
___	___	___	___	___	___
___	___	___	___	___	___
___	___	___	___	___	___
___	___	___	___	___	___
___	___	___	___	___	___
___	___	___	___	___	___
___	___	___	___	___	___
___	___	___	___	___	___

Next, in a column beneath the letter T, write the rest of the alphabet in order. When you get to Z, continue with A and keep going until you finish with S. Do this with each of the letters you wrote. So, the column under the letter T begins with U, is followed by V, and so on. The column under C begins with D, is followed by E, and continues. A sample is shown for you.

Once you have run through the alphabet under the first six letters in the code, look through the combinations of letters until you find one that spells words. One of the combinations will spell "FOR THE." Now you know that T stands for F, C stands for H, and so forth.

Next, write the letters of the alphabet in order from left to right, the way you would normally see them. Above the F, place a T. Next, above the O write the letter C. Continue through the alphabet. The top row are the code letters, the bottom row is the alphabet. To crack the code, look at the top row for the letter in the message and match it to the letter below it in the alphabet. Now you have the code and can decipher the message.

T C

A B C D E **F** G H I J K L M N **O** P Q R S T U V W X Y Z

TCF HVS ASGGOUS CT HVS QFCGG WG

TCCZWGVBSGG HC HVCGS KVC OFS DSFWGVWBU,

PIH HC IG KVC OFS PSWBU GOJSR WH WG

HVS DCKSF CT UCR.

1 CORINTHIANS 1:18

The truth of this message for God's Secret Agents is clear: the source of our power is God's love made perfect in Jesus. Others may want to rely on themselves. But through faith, we rely on Jesus.

Strength and Power

You have a power that the rest of the world may never understand. To reveal the power source identified in the message below, use the shifted alphabet code. Write the first eight letters of the encoded message as shown in the sample below.

MFE ESZDP HSZ SZAP TY ESP WZCO HTWW

M	F	E	E	S	Z	D	P
N	G	F	F	T	A	E	Q
O	H	G	G	U	B	F	R
P	I	H	H	V	C	G	S
Q	J	I	I	W	D	H	T
R	K	J	J	X	E	I	U
S	L	K	K	Y	F	J	V
___	___	___	___	___	___	___	___
___	___	___	___	___	___	___	___
___	___	___	___	___	___	___	___
___	___	___	___	___	___	___	___
___	___	___	___	___	___	___	___
___	___	___	___	___	___	___	___
___	___	___	___	___	___	___	___
___	___	___	___	___	___	___	___
___	___	___	___	___	___	___	___
___	___	___	___	___	___	___	___
___	___	___	___	___	___	___	___
___	___	___	___	___	___	___	___
___	___	___	___	___	___	___	___

Next, in a column beneath the letter M, write the rest of the alphabet in order. When you get to Z, continue with A and keep going until you finish with L. Do this with each of the letters you wrote. So, the column under the letter M begins with N, is followed by O, and so on. The column under F begins with G, is followed by H, and continues. A sample is shown for you.

Once you have run through the alphabet under the first five letters in the code, look through the combinations of letters until you find one that spells words. One of the combinations will spell "BUT THOSE." Now you know that M stands for B, F stands for U, and so forth.

Next, write the letters of the alphabet in order from left to right, the way you would normally see them. Above the B, place an M. Next, above the U write the letter F. Continue through the alphabet. The top row are the code letters, the bottom row is the alphabet. To crack the code, look at the top row for the letter in the message and match it to the letter below it in the alphabet. Now you have the code and can decipher the message.

M																			F						
A	**B**	C	D	E	F	G	H	I	J	K	L	M	N	O	P	Q	R	S	T	**U**	V	W	X	Y	Z

MFE ESZDP HSZ SZAP TY ESP WZCO

HTWW CPYPH ESPTC DECPYRES. ESPJ HTWW

DZLC ZY HTYRD WTVP PLRWPD; ESPJ HTWW

CFY LYO YZE RCZH HPLCJ, ESPJ HTWW

HLWV LYO YZE MP QLTYE.

ISAIAH 40:31

To help you further understand these messages, check out these passages: 1 Peter 5:11, 1 Corinthians 1:18, and Isaiah 40:31.

Finding the Answers

Some secret messages include a code, but others do not. This message does not come with a decoder. Instead, you will create it. Turn to 2 Timothy 3:16. Write the Bible verse, letter by letter, under the pictures. There will be some blank spaces. When you have matched all the letters to pictures, you will have created the code. Use this code to decipher the rest of the messages.

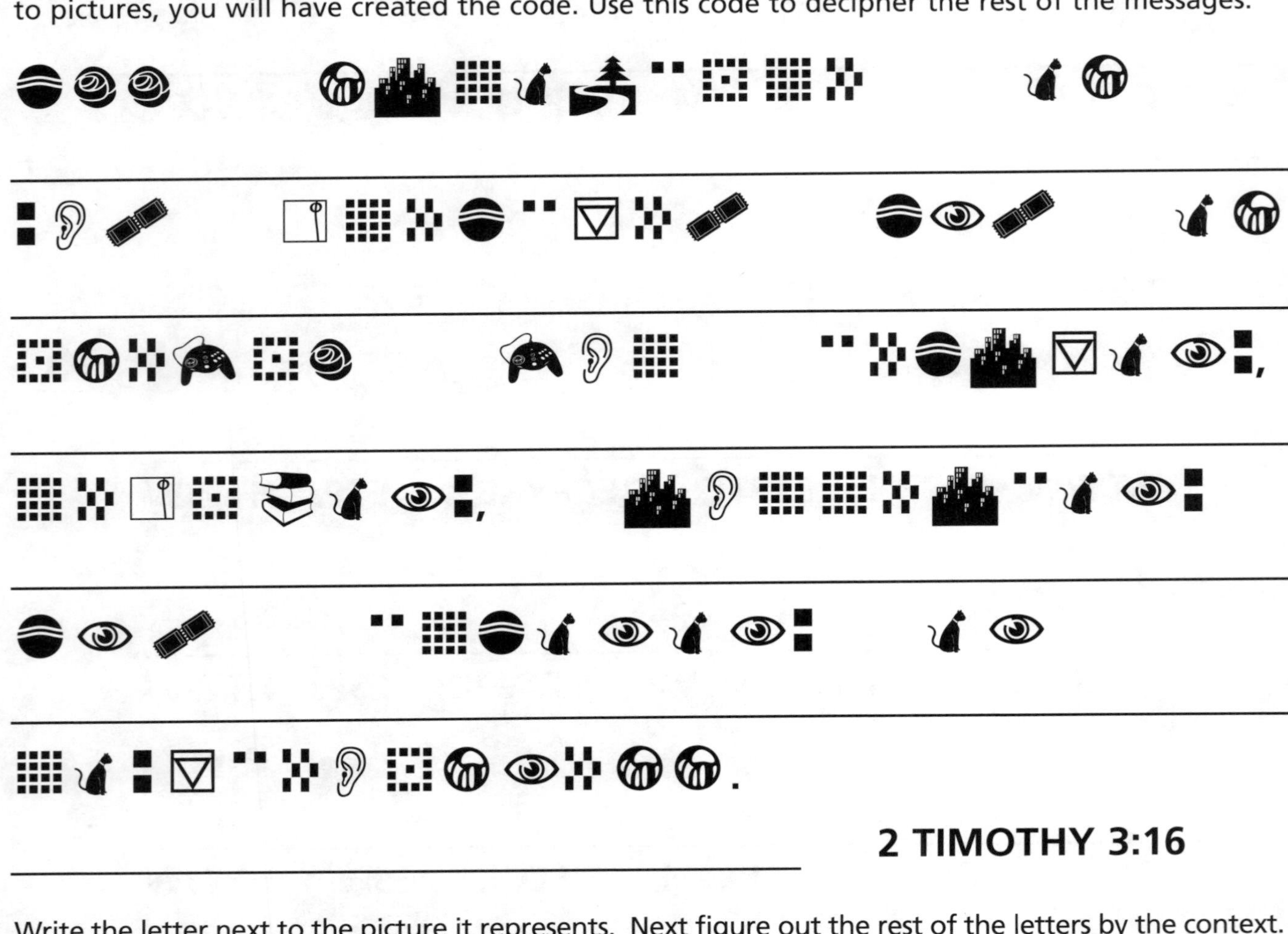

2 TIMOTHY 3:16

Write the letter next to the picture it represents. Next figure out the rest of the letters by the context.

Now use the code to reveal these hidden messages.

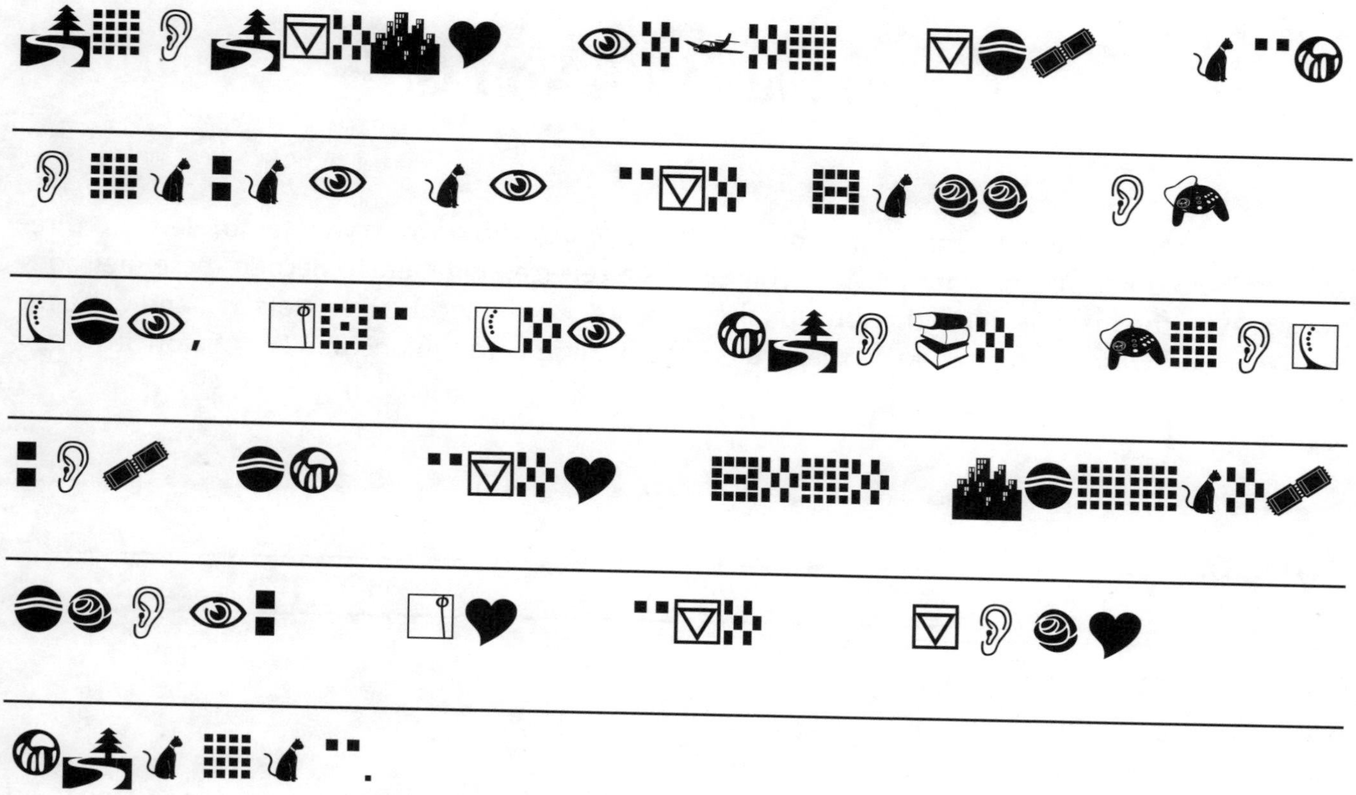

2 PETER 1:21

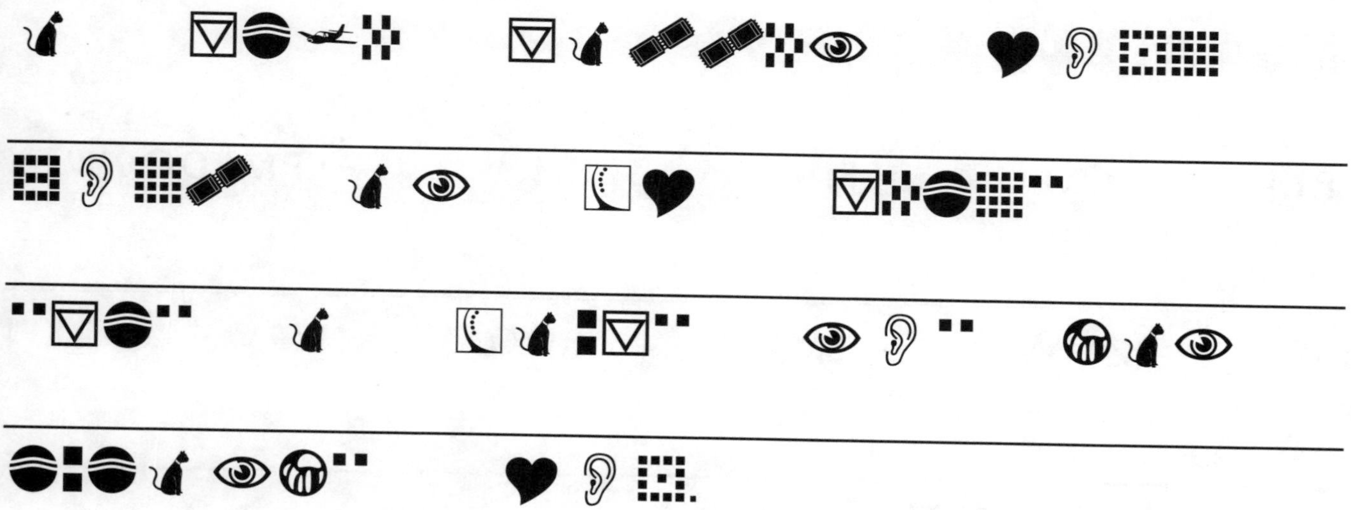

PSALM 119:11

Breaking codes and sharing the Good News of Jesus is easier when you know where to begin. With God as the source of the truth you share with others, you will always begin in the right place!

Which Way Will You Go?

As a Secret Agent begins a mission, it is important to know which way to go. Here are three clues to help guide you on your mission. This code is a reverse alphabet. To decode these messages, start at A on the first line and write the alphabet forward. On the second line, start at Z and write the alphabet backward. Be sure to write the letters so they align with the one above or below it.

A ______________________________

Z ______________________________

To reveal the clues, match the letters in the code above with the words in the message below, and write them in the space provided.

RM ZOO BLFI DZBH ZXPMLDOVWTV

____

SRN, ZMW SV DROO NZPV BLFI

____

KZGSH HGIZRTSG.

____

PROVERBS 3:6

R DROO TL YVULIV BLF ZMW DROO

OVEVO GSV NLFMGZRMH; R DROO YIVZP

WLDM TZGVH LU YILMAV ZMW XFG

GSILFTS YZIH LU RILM.

ISAIAH 45:20

R DROO RMHGIFXG BLF ZMW GVZXS

BLF RM GSV DZB BLF HSLFOW TL;

R DROO XLFMHVO BLF ZMW DZGXS

LEVI BLF.

PSALM 32:8

Read John 10:27. Jesus, the Good Shepherd, will always lead us along the right path!

Secrets

To decode these top-secret messages, you will need a New International Version of the Bible. First, find the verses listed here. Use the number in parentheses to count the words in the verse to find the word you need. Count carefully to get the right message. Write the word in the space provided. When you have all the words, you have the top-secret message. **Hint:** Hyphenated words and words that are divided at the end of the line count as one.

2 Corinthians 5:7 (1) Exodus 4:12 (7) Revelation 22:21 (3) Job 37:5 (1)

____________ ____________ ____________ ____________

Deuteronomy 29:29 (2) James 1:5 (6).

____________ ____________ **1 CORINTHIANS 2:7**

Jeremiah 33:3 (5) Leviticus 25:18 (13) Isaiah 7:14 (18) Psalm 55:22 (11) Psalm 34:15 (8)

____________ ____________ ____________ ____________ ____________

Proverbs 10:2 (2) James 3:18 (9) Psalm 18:28 (12), 1 Kings 10:23 (6) Colossians 1:5 (12)

____________ ____________ ____________ ____________ ____________

2 Corinthians 5:17 (5) Matthew 6:6 (29) Jeremiah 23:24 (6).

____________ ____________ ____________ **ISAIAH 45:3**

You have a very special secret in this next code. Why do you think this secret has been given to you?

"1 Corinthians 2:12 (11) 1 Corinthians 2:7 (6) Galatians 5:22 (4) 1 Peter 3:4 (10)

____________ ____________ ____________ ____________

2 Samuel 7:12 (33) Acts 13:38 (14) 2 Chronicles 36:15 (4) John 5:24 (16)

____________ ____________ ____________ ____________

Luke 2:11 (10) Matthew 6:33 (15) John 14:21 (34) Psalm 31:24 (7)."

____________ ____________ ____________ ____________ **MARK 4:11**

What do we do with these secrets?

Psalm 42:1 (9) **Psalm 61:8 (1),** **Psalm 36:7 (12)** **Romans 8:26 (18)** **Jeremiah 29:11 (14)**

_____________ _____________ _____________ _____________ _____________

Job 37:24 (10) **1 John 4:7 (4)** **Psalm 103:11 (4)** **Psalm 34:22 (5)** **Hebrews 11:1 (6)**

_____________ _____________ _____________ _____________ _____________

Galatians 3:26 (10) **Jeremiah 33:3 (4)** **Isaiah 66:13 (1)** **Acts 2:41 (1)**

_____________ _____________ _____________ _____________

Matthew 25:20 (17) **Philippians 4:6 (14)** **Colossians 4:5 (11)** **Philippians 4:12 (23)**

_____________ _____________ _____________ _____________

2 Samuel 7:28 (17) **Matthew 12:50 (6)** **John 3:16 (2).**

_____________ _____________ _____________ **1 CORINTHIANS 4:1**

God's Good News is a special kind of secret—one that He wants us to share with everyone. Find a friend who doesn't know Jesus and tell him about God's love and the salvation that is ours through Jesus' death and resurrection. You can do this in code or tell him plainly.

Key Word Connection

It is important for Secret Agents to keep communicating with the command unit. The following messages will help you to keep in touch with the right command unit. To crack this code, use the key word COMMUNICATION. Write it on a piece of paper, then cross out all the letters that are used twice. Next, write the alphabet across the page. Put the C in COMMUNICATION above the A in the alphabet. Write O over B and M over C. Continue until all the letters in the key word are used. Then fill in the rest of the line with the alphabet letters you haven't used yet. The first few letters are shown to help you get started.

C O M ~~M~~ U N I ~~C~~ A T ~~I O N~~

C O M U __________________________________

A B C ___________________________________

Now you have the code to decipher this message. Remember, the top row of letters is the code, the bottom row is the alphabet. Match the letters below with the correct alphabet letters and decipher the message.

MCFF RJ GN CHU B WBFF CHQWNP

____

YJS CHU RNFF YJS APNCR CHU

____

SHQNCPMTCOFN RTBHAQ YJS UJ HJR

____

EHJW.

____________________ **JEREMIAH 33:3**

How do you stay in touch with God? Discover one way in Colossians 4:2–3.

Another Key Word Connection

As a Secret Agent, making the right connections will keep you on the right track. Make your connection by cracking this code. Write the word PRAYER on a piece of paper, then cross out all the letters that are used twice. Next, write the alphabet across the page. Put the P in PRAYER above the A in the alphabet. Write R over B and A over C. Continue until all the letters in the key word are used. Then fill in the rest of the line with the alphabet letters you haven't used yet. The first few letters are done for you.

PRAYE~~R~~

P R A Y E B C ______________________________________
A B C ____

Now you have the code to decipher this message. Remember, the top row of letters is the code, the bottom row is the alphabet. Match the letters below with the code and read the hidden message.

"FB XLT REIFEUE, XLT VFII OEAEFUE

____

VDPSEUEO XLT PQH BLO FK MOPXEO."

____

________________________ **MATTHEW 21:22**

Your connection to God the Father is Jesus. Pray in His name; God the Father will hear you. And He promises to answer your prayers in the way that is best for you, according to His will.

Phrase that Pays

Secret Agents often use code words or phrases to identify themselves. The phrase in the hidden message below would be a great one for God's Secret Agents. To crack this code, use TALK TO GOD as the key words. Cross out all the letters that are used twice. Next, write the alphabet on the second line below. Put the T in TALK TO GOD above the A in the alphabet. Write A over B and L over C. Continue until all the letters in the key word are used. Then fill in the rest of the line with the alphabet letters you haven't used yet. **Hint:** After you've written all the letters in the key word, you'll begin the code with B.

TALK TO GOD

T A L ____

A B C D E F G H I J K L M N O P Q R S T U V W X Y Z

Now you have the code to decipher this message. Remember, the top row of letters is the code, the bottom row is the alphabet. Match the coded letters with the correct alphabet letters and read the hidden message.

"TRF TJK CS WCHH AO DCVOJ SM

____

YMU; ROOF TJK YMU WCHH GCJK;

____

FJMLF TJK SBO KMMQ WCHH AO

____

MNOJOK SM YMU."

____

MATTHEW 7:7

Why not make a Secret Agent sign that reads "ASK, SEEK, KNOCK"? Turn to Matthew 7:8–12 to read more about prayer.

Keeping in Touch

Secret Agents need to know that their connections will be crystal clear. To crack this code, use CLARITY as the key word. Write it on a piece of paper, then cross out any letters that are used twice. Next, write the alphabet across the page. Put the C in CLARITY above the A in the alphabet. Write L over B and A over C. Continue until all the letters in the key word are used. Then fill in the rest of the line with the alphabet letters you haven't used yet. It should look like this:

CLARITY

C L A _______________________________________

A B C _______________________________________

Now you have the code you need to decipher this message. Remember, the top row of letters is the code, the bottom row is the alphabet. Match the coded letters with the correct alphabet letters and read the hidden message.

LITKOI QBIX ACGG D VDGG CJPVIO;

____

VBDGI QBIX COI PQDGG PMICFDJY D

____

VDGG BICO.

_____________________ **ISAIAH 65:24**

Look up Isaiah 65:23 to read more about God's promises to know our needs and to listen to our prayers.

Chart Your Course

God provides you with all you need to carry out His mission. He supplies the protection, power, and direction. He helps you get ready to do all you can so the Good News of the Gospel can be spread. To decode the following message, you will need the chart below.

	1	2	3	4	5	6	7	8	9	10	11	12	13	14	15	16	17	18	19	20	21	22	23	24	25	26
1	**A**	**B**	**C**	**D**	**E**	**F**	**G**	**H**	**I**	**J**	**K**	**L**	**M**	**N**	**O**	**P**	**Q**	**R**	**S**	**T**	**U**	**V**	**W**	**X**	**Y**	**Z**
2	B	C	D	E	F	G	H	I	J	K	L	M	N	O	P	Q	R	S	T	U	V	W	X	Y	Z	A
3	C	D	E	F	G	H	I	J	K	L	M	N	O	P	Q	R	S	T	U	V	W	X	Y	Z	A	B
4	D	E	F	G	H	I	J	K	L	M	N	O	P	Q	R	S	T	U	V	W	X	Y	Z	A	B	C
5	E	F	G	H	I	J	K	L	M	N	O	P	Q	R	S	T	U	V	W	X	Y	Z	A	B	C	D
6	F	G	H	I	J	K	L	M	N	O	P	Q	R	S	T	U	V	W	X	Y	Z	A	B	C	D	E
7	G	H	I	J	K	L	M	N	O	P	Q	R	S	T	U	V	W	X	Y	Z	A	B	C	D	E	F
8	H	I	J	K	L	M	N	O	P	Q	R	S	T	U	V	W	X	Y	Z	A	B	C	D	E	F	G
9	I	J	K	L	M	N	O	P	Q	R	S	T	U	V	W	X	Y	Z	A	B	C	D	E	F	G	H
10	J	K	L	M	N	O	P	Q	R	S	T	U	V	W	X	Y	Z	A	B	C	D	E	F	G	H	I
11	K	L	M	N	O	P	Q	R	S	T	U	V	W	X	Y	Z	A	B	C	D	E	F	G	H	I	J
12	L	M	N	O	P	Q	R	S	T	U	V	W	X	Y	Z	A	B	C	D	E	F	G	H	I	J	K
13	M	N	O	P	Q	R	S	T	U	V	W	X	Y	Z	A	B	C	D	E	F	G	H	I	J	K	L
14	N	O	P	Q	R	S	T	U	V	W	X	Y	Z	A	B	C	D	E	F	G	H	I	J	K	L	M
15	O	P	Q	R	S	T	U	V	W	X	Y	Z	A	B	C	D	E	F	G	H	I	J	K	L	M	N
16	P	Q	R	S	T	U	V	W	X	Y	Z	A	B	C	D	E	F	G	H	I	J	K	L	M	N	O
17	Q	R	S	T	U	V	W	X	Y	Z	A	B	C	D	E	F	G	H	I	J	K	L	M	N	O	P
18	R	S	T	U	V	W	X	Y	Z	A	B	C	D	E	F	G	H	I	J	K	L	M	N	O	P	Q
19	S	T	U	V	W	X	Y	Z	A	B	C	D	E	F	G	H	I	J	K	L	M	N	O	P	Q	R
20	T	U	V	W	X	Y	Z	A	B	C	D	E	F	G	H	I	J	K	L	M	N	O	P	Q	R	S
21	U	V	W	X	Y	Z	A	B	C	D	E	F	G	H	I	J	K	L	M	N	O	P	Q	R	S	T
22	V	W	X	Y	Z	A	B	C	D	E	F	G	H	I	J	K	L	M	N	O	P	Q	R	S	T	U
23	W	X	Y	Z	A	B	C	D	E	F	G	H	I	J	K	L	M	N	O	P	Q	R	S	T	U	V
24	X	Y	Z	A	B	C	D	E	F	G	H	I	J	K	L	M	N	O	P	Q	R	S	T	U	V	W
25	Y	Z	A	B	C	D	E	F	G	H	I	J	K	L	M	N	O	P	Q	R	S	T	U	V	W	X
26	Z	A	B	C	D	E	F	G	H	I	J	K	L	M	N	O	P	Q	R	S	T	U	V	W	X	Y

This is a difficult code, but it holds important information about your mission. The first letter in this code is also the first letter in the message (T=T). To find the second letter, find that letter in the second row and match it to the letter straight above it in the top row. (I=H) To find the third letter, find that letter in the third row and follow it up to the top row. (G=E) So far we have THE. Keep going through the message until you get to the bottom of the chart, then start at the top again. Always use the top row of the chart as your key. **Hint:** It will help to number the letters and rows. Then, if you lose your place, you can find the corresponding row to the letter you are on. Use a ruler to keep your rows straight.

1 2 3 4 5 6 7 8 9 10 11 12 13 14 15 16 17 18 19 20 21 22 23 24 25 26 1 2 3

T I G U I K U Y M P Y L Z Q A P A V V B M X E M J D S PH

____

DPQ THBRYYE, OOEJZRBHB PECL IO VKI

____

SGTM XP ETR TPJYWK UIZ LD SHF URR

____

FTK WO DSQ UCAO JHBLDP.

____

MATTHEW 28:19

This message involves recruiting more Secret Agents in God's name.
See Matthew 28:20 for additional instructions.

Two-Part Message

This message about your mission as God's Secret Agent comes in two parts. Use the chart below to decode it.

1	**A**	**B**	**C**	**D**	**E**	**F**	**G**	**H**	**I**	**J**	**K**	**L**	**M**	**N**	**O**	**P**	**Q**	**R**	**S**	**T**	**U**	**V**	**W**	**X**	**Y**	**Z**
2	B	C	D	E	F	G	H	I	J	K	L	M	N	O	P	Q	R	S	T	U	V	W	X	Y	Z	A
3	C	D	E	F	G	H	I	J	K	L	M	N	O	P	Q	R	S	T	U	V	W	X	Y	Z	A	B
4	D	E	F	G	H	I	J	K	L	M	N	O	P	Q	R	S	T	U	V	W	X	Y	Z	A	B	C
5	E	F	G	H	I	J	K	L	M	N	O	P	Q	R	S	T	U	V	W	X	Y	Z	A	B	C	D
6	F	G	H	I	J	K	L	M	N	O	P	Q	R	S	T	U	V	W	X	Y	Z	A	B	C	D	E
7	G	H	I	J	K	L	M	N	O	P	Q	R	S	T	U	V	W	X	Y	Z	A	B	C	D	E	F
8	H	I	J	K	L	M	N	O	P	Q	R	S	T	U	V	W	X	Y	Z	A	B	C	D	E	F	G
9	I	J	K	L	M	N	O	P	Q	R	S	T	U	V	W	X	Y	Z	A	B	C	D	E	F	G	H
10	J	K	L	M	N	O	P	Q	R	S	T	U	V	W	X	Y	Z	A	B	C	D	E	F	G	H	I
11	K	L	M	N	O	P	Q	R	S	T	U	V	W	X	Y	Z	A	B	C	D	E	F	G	H	I	J
12	L	M	N	O	P	Q	R	S	T	U	V	W	X	Y	Z	A	B	C	D	E	F	G	H	I	J	K
13	M	N	O	P	Q	R	S	T	U	V	W	X	Y	Z	A	B	C	D	E	F	G	H	I	J	K	L
14	N	O	P	Q	R	S	T	U	V	W	X	Y	Z	A	B	C	D	E	F	G	H	I	J	K	L	M
15	O	P	Q	R	S	T	U	V	W	X	Y	Z	A	B	C	D	E	F	G	H	I	J	K	L	M	N
16	P	Q	R	S	T	U	V	W	X	Y	Z	A	B	C	D	E	F	G	H	I	J	K	L	M	N	O
17	Q	R	S	T	U	V	W	X	Y	Z	A	B	C	D	E	F	G	H	I	J	K	L	M	N	O	P
18	R	S	T	U	V	W	X	Y	Z	A	B	C	D	E	F	G	H	I	J	K	L	M	N	O	P	Q
19	S	T	U	V	W	X	Y	Z	A	B	C	D	E	F	G	H	I	J	K	L	M	N	O	P	Q	R
20	T	U	V	W	X	Y	Z	A	B	C	D	E	F	G	H	I	J	K	L	M	N	O	P	Q	R	S
21	U	V	W	X	Y	Z	A	B	C	D	E	F	G	H	I	J	K	L	M	N	O	P	Q	R	S	T
22	V	W	X	Y	Z	A	B	C	D	E	F	G	H	I	J	K	L	M	N	O	P	Q	R	S	T	U
23	W	X	Y	Z	A	B	C	D	E	F	G	H	I	J	K	L	M	N	O	P	Q	R	S	T	U	V
24	X	Y	Z	A	B	C	D	E	F	G	H	I	J	K	L	M	N	O	P	Q	R	S	T	U	V	W
25	Y	Z	A	B	C	D	E	F	G	H	I	J	K	L	M	N	O	P	Q	R	S	T	U	V	W	X
26	Z	A	B	C	D	E	F	G	H	I	J	K	L	M	N	O	P	Q	R	S	T	U	V	W	X	Y

This is a difficult code, but it holds important information about your mission. The first letter in this code is G. To find the second letter, find that letter in the second row and match it to the letter straight above it in the top row. (P=O) To find the third letter, find that letter in the third row and follow it up to the top row. (K=I) So far we have GO I. Keep going through the message until you get to the bottom of the chart, then start at the top again. Always use the top row of the chart as your key. **Hint:** It will help to number the letters and rows. Then, if you lose your place, you can find the corresponding row to the letter you are on. Use a ruler to keep your rows straight.

1 2 3 4 5 6 7 8 9 10 11 12 13 14 15 16 17 18 19 20 21 22 23 24 25 26

"GP KQXT GST CRP IBFAT RFW JMAXAG

____

TIG JSTJ UMFC EA NZA SIWTNDKK."

______________________________________ **MARK 16:15**

"LPXH IFIO WCRPD."

______________________________________ **JOHN 15:17**

All of God's Secret Agents are given this special mission. What can you ask God to help you do today to get you started on your way?

Tips for Teachers

Use these games in your classroom to encourage students to think like God's Secret Agents. Feel free to change and adapt according to the age group and setting.

I Spy. Seat students in a circle, indoors or out. Tell them, "I am going to give you clues about something I see. When you think you know what I'm talking about, raise your hand." Then say, "I spy something (green that moves in the breeze and hangs from tree branches)." Let students guess until someone suggests you "spy" a leaf. You can use this as an ice-breaker or get-acquainted game. Substitute *someone* for *something* and describe one of the students. When students are comfortable with the concept of this game, let them take turns giving clues.

Mystery Objects. Write names of common objects on small slips of paper, one item per slip (for example: book, bicycle, pencil, television). Fold the slips in half and place them in a shoebox, bowl, or other container. Divide the class into two teams. Choose a student from each team to draw a slip of paper from the box. Give the student a moment or two to think about how this object looks. He or she will then give three clues to describe the object. (For example: This object is square. It is made of glass and wood or plastic. It makes sounds.) Both teams have 20 seconds to discuss quietly what they think the object is. When they decide on an answer, they are to raise their hands. Each team gets one guess. The first team that correctly names the object earns 10 points. Let someone from the other team draw a slip of paper and give clues. Play continues until one team has earned 50 points.

Detectives' Dilemma. Make an audio recording of a variety of common sounds, such as water running from a faucet, a car engine starting, footsteps, a door closing, keys rattling, and so on. As you record the sounds, leave a few moments of silence between each sound. Divide the class into two teams. As you play each sound, team members quietly confer about the origin of the sound. When a team can identify the sound, members raise their hands. Correct guesses earn 10 points. The team with the most points at the end of the game wins.

Mystery Pictures. You will need a chalkboard and chalk, strips of paper, a pencil, and a hat or box. List clues of common objects on the pieces of paper (for example: car, computer, magnifying glass), one clue per slip. Fold the slips in half and place them in the hat or box. Select someone to be an artist. The artist selects a slip of paper, then draws a picture of the clue on the chalkboard. The rest of the students try to guess what the artist has drawn. The first student to correctly guess the object becomes the artist for the next round. If no one guesses correctly, the artist selects another slip of paper and draws again.

Mystery Chalk Outlines. You will need sidewalk chalk and items to trace (select items that have distinctive shapes and sizes, such as a ruler, large rubber band, hand, fork, spoon, pear, etc.). Before the game begins, trace around the items with chalk on a hard surface. Challenge students to correctly guess the identity of the outlines. Or make chalk outlines of each child and let students guess the identities.

Who's Changed? Select a student to be "It." While "It" watches carefully, the other students scatter across the play area. "It" says, "Freeze," and all stop and hold a pose as if frozen. "It" turns his or her back to the group. One student changes his or her pose. "It" turns around and tries to identify who changed. If "It" guesses correctly, he or she exchanges places with the changed person. If "It" guesses incorrectly, all students except the changer gradually move to one side to help "It" identify the changer.

What's the Clue? You will need a drawstring bag made of cloth that cannot be seen through, clue items with unique textures, sizes, and shapes (for example, a beaded necklace, sandpaper, nickel, button, sponge, small piece of carpet, dental floss). Place one item in the bag. Select a student to reach inside the bag to touch the object. Have the student give clues that describe the object without naming it. Take turns until each student has a chance.

Progressive Evidence. To play this game, you will need a list of common items and pencils for each team or each student. Make a list of items to find in your classroom, school, or play area. Items might include a fire extinguisher, flag, picture of Jesus, cross, basketball, etc. Assign each item a point value (e.g. 1 point for very easy-to-find items, 5 points for somewhat easy-to-find items, 10 points for hard-to-find items). Hand out lists to individual students or teams and challenge them to locate items within a specified time. Students should write locations next to the item name on the list. No items should be collected or moved.

Disappearing Bible Words. Print John 14:6 on the chalkboard or dry-erase board. Read the verse aloud together. Make these points to introduce the memory game:

- John the Baptist testified that Jesus takes away the sins of the world and that He is God's Son.
- Jesus proved it when He died on the cross and came alive again. He defeated sin, death, and Satan and opened heaven's gate for us. Believing that Jesus is our Savior is the only way to heaven. Jesus is the Way, the Truth, and the Life.
- We can test our memory skills by remembering facts.

Repeat the verse aloud once more, then erase two words at a time from different parts of the verse. After each erasure of words, have students say the entire verse together again. Continue erasing. Students will say the entire verse from memory.

Evidence Seekers. You will need 20 or more objects to hide (for example, hats, scarves, books, toys, costume jewelry) and a large box or trunk. Before the game begins, divide students into teams of two or three. Send one team out of the room. Hide the objects around the classroom or play area. Ask the students to come back into the room. Give them a list of the hidden objects. Give them a time limit of seven minutes and let them work together to locate the hidden items. As each item is found, students place it in the box or chest. The game ends when all items are found or when the time limit is up. If time ends before all the items are found, give clues to help the team find the missing objects. Continue until all teams have a chance to look for evidence.

Make the fun last with these recipes that are easy to do in any classroom.

Invisible Ink. Dip a narrow-tip brush in citrus juice to paint a short Bible verse or prayer on white paper. Let dry. Hold the paper over a light bulb until the juice turns brown to reveal the message. Take care not to burn the paper.

Disappearing Ink. Mix well equal parts of water, iodine, and all-purpose cooking starch. It will look like blue-black ink. Use a narrow-tip brush to paint a short Bible verse or prayer on white paper. In about three days the ink will completely disappear.

Puzzling Sandwiches. You will need sandwiches, cookie cutters, knives, small paper plates. Make a sandwich for each student. Cheese or peanut butter on firm bread, such as whole wheat or sourdough, work best. Use a cookie cutter and knife to cut the sandwich into five or six puzzle pieces. Serve jumbled on a small paper plates. Have children put the puzzle pieces together before eating.

Mystery Cake. You will need 1 white cake mix prepared according to directions on the package, food coloring, 4 8-inch cake pans, 4 bowls, 2 16-oz. cans of white frosting, colorful cake decorating gel. Mix cake according to package directions to make batter. Divide batter equally into four bowls, about 1 cup of batter in each. Mix a different color of food coloring into the batter in each bowl. Pour batter into four greased and floured pans. Bake about 15 minutes at 350 degrees until done. Let layers cool completely. Assemble cake by spreading frosting between each layer and on top and sides of cake. Decorate with gel. The cut cake will reveal a colorful surprise. Option: add food coloring to frosting too.

Answers

Page 8—In the day of my trouble I will call to You, for You will answer me. Psalm 86:7

Page 9—My help comes from the LORD, the Maker of heaven and earth. Psalm 121:2

Page 10—Even though I walk through the valley of the shadow of death, I will fear no evil, for You are with me. Psalm 23:4

Page 11—God is our refuge and strength, an ever-present help in trouble. Psalm 46:1

Page 12—Put on the full armor of God so that you can take your stand against the devil's schemes. Ephesians 6:11

Page 13—Stand firm then, with the belt of truth buckled around your waist, with the breastplate of righteousness in place. Ephesians 6:14

Page 14—But let all who take refuge in You be glad; let them ever sing for joy. … Those who love Your name may rejoice in You. Psalm 5:11

Page 15—For He will command His angels concerning you to guard you in all your ways. Psalm 91:11

Page 16—My help comes from the LORD, the Maker of heaven and earth. Psalm 121:2

Jesus answered, "I am the Way and the Truth and the Life. No one comes to the Father except through Me." John 14:6

Page 17—Give ear to my words, O LORD consider my sighing. Listen to my cry for help, my King and my God, for to You I pray. In the morning, O LORD, You hear my voice; in the morning I lay my requests before You and wait in expectation. Psalm 5:1–3

"No eye has seen, no ear has heard no mind has conceived what God has prepared for those who love Him." 1 Corinthians 2:9

Page 20—Taste and see that the LORD is good. Psalm 34:8

Come and see what God has done, how awesome His works in man's behalf! Psalm 66:5

Open my eyes that I may see wonderful things in Your law. Psalm 119:18

"No one can see the kingdom of God unless he is born again." John 3:3

"Blessed are the pure in heart, for they will see God." Matthew 5:8

Page 22—Everyone who calls on the name of the LORD will be saved. Joel 2:32

Page 23—And this is what He promised us—even eternal life. 1 John 2:25

For it is by grace you have been saved, through faith and this not from yourselves—it is the gift of God—not by works, so that no one can boast. Ephesians 2:8–9

Page 24—The Lord is my strength and my song; He has become my salvation. He is my God and I will praise Him, my father's God, and I will exalt Him. Exodus 15:2

Page 25—FOR|GO DISO|LO VED|TH E|WORL D|THAT| HE|GAV E|HIS|O NE|AND| ONLY|S ON|THA T|WHOE VER|BE LIEVE S|IN|HI M|SHAL L|NOT|P ERISH|BUT|HA VE|ETE RNAL|L IFE

"For God so loved the world that He gave His one and only Son, that whoever believes in Him shall not perish but have eternal life." John 3:16

Page 26—FOR|WH OEVER| WANTS| TO|SAV E|HIS|L IFE|WI LL|LOS E|IT|BU T|WHOE VER|LO SES|HI S|LIFE| FOR|ME| AND|FO R|THE|G OSPEL| WILL|S AVE|IT

"For whoever wants to save his life will lose it, but whoever loses his life for Me and for the Gospel will save it." Mark 8:35

Page 27—"A farmer went out to sow his seed. As he was scattering the seed, some fell along the path, and the birds came and ate it up. Some fell on rocky places, where it did not have much soil. It sprang up quickly, because the soil was shallow. But when the sun came up, the plants were scorched, and they withered because they had no root. Other seed fell among thorns, which grew up and choked the plants. Still other seed fell on good soil, where it produced a crop—a hundred, sixty or thirty times what was sown. He who has ears, let him hear." Matthew 13:3–9

Page 28— I have hidden Your word in my heart that I might not sin against You. Psalm 119:11

Page 29— DTEHLEILGOHRTDYWOIULRLSOEPLEFNITNHTEHHEELAOVREDNASNTDHHEESWTIOLRL EGHIOVUESYEOOUFTHHIESDBEOSUINRTEYSTOOFSYEONUDRRHAEIANROT

Delight yourself in the Lord and He will give you the desires of your heart. Psalm 37:4

TNHYEOLUORRLDAGNIDVIENSSSETARSEONNGATNHDTTOOHBILSEPSESOAPLLLETTHH EEWLOORRKDOBFLYEOSUSREHSAHNIDSSPYEOOUPWLIELWLILTEHNPDETAOCME

The Lord gives strength to His people; the Lord blesses His people with peace. Psalm 29:11

Page 30—For the Lord gives wisdom, and from His mouth come knowledge and understanding. Proverbs 2:6

And my God will meet all your needs according to His glorious riches in Christ Jesus. Philippians 4:19

For the Lord God is a sun and shield; the Lord bestows favor and honor; no good thing does He withhold from those whose walk is blameless. Psalm 84:11

The Lord will open the heavens, the storehouse of His bounty, to send rain on your land in season and to bless all the work of your hands. You will lend to many nations but will borrow from none. The Lord will make you the head, not the tail. If you pay attention to the commands of the Lord your God that I give you this day and carefully follow them, you will always be at the top, never at the bottom. Do not turn aside from any of the commands I give you today. Deuteronomy 28:12–14

Page 33—"The Counselor, the Holy Spirit, whom the Father will send in My name, will teach you all things and will remind you of everything I have said to you." John 14:26

"But you will receive power when the Holy Spirit comes on you." Acts 1:8

The Spirit searches all things, even the deep things of God. 1 Corinthians 2:10

May the God of hope fill you with all joy and peace as you trust in Him, so that you may overflow with hope by the power of the Holy Spirit. Romans 15:13

Page 34—

L	FDQ	GR
M	GER	HS
N	HFS	IT
O	IGT	JU
P	JHU	KV
Q	KIV	LW
R	LJW	MX
S	MKX	NY
T	NLY	OZ
U	OMZ	PA
V	PNA	QB
W	QOB	RC
X	RPC	SD
Y	SQD	TE
Z	TRE	UF
A	USF	VG
B	VTG	WH
C	WUH	XI
D	XVI	YJ
E	YWJ	ZK
F	ZXK	AL
G	AYL	BM
H	BZM	CN
I	**CAN**	**DO**
J	DBO	EP
K	ECP	FQ

D E F G H I J K L M N O P Q R S T U V W X Y Z A B C
A B C D E F G H I J K L M N O P Q R S T U V W X Y Z

I can do everything through Him who gives me strength. Philippians 4:13

Page 36—

A B C D E F G H I J K L M N O P Q R S T U V W X Y Z
Z Y X W V U T S R Q P O N M L K J I H G F E D C A B

You have made known to me the path of life; You will fill me with joy in Your presence, with eternal pleasures at Your right hand. Psalm 16:11

Don't let anyone look down on you because you are young, but set an example for the believers in speech, in life, in love, in faith and in purity. 1 Timothy 4:12

Page 37—

OJ	CDH
PK	DEI
QL	EFJ
RM	FGK
SN	GHL
TO	**HIM**
UP	IJN

V W X Y Z A B C D E F G H I J K L M N O P Q R S T U
A B C D E F G H I J K L M N O P Q R S T U V W X Y Z

To Him be the power for ever and ever. Amen. 1 Peter 5:11

*

Page 39—

T C F	H U S
U D G	I W T
V E H	J X U
W F I	K Y V
X G J	L Z W
Y H K	M A X
Z I L	N B Y
A J M	O C Z
B K N	P D A
C L O	Q E B
D M P	R F C
E N Q	S G D
F O R	**T H E**
G P S	U I F
H Q T	V J G

O P Q R S T U V W X Y Z A B C D E F G H I J K L M N
A B C D E F G H I J K L M N O P Q R S T U V W X Y Z

For the message of the cross is foolishness to those who are perishing, but to us who are being saved it is the power of God. 1 Corinthians 1:18

Page 41—

M F E	E S Z D P
N G F	F T A E Q
O H G	G U B F R
P I H	H V C G S
Q J I	I W D H T
R K J	J X E I U
S L K	K Y F J V
T M L	L Z G K W
U N M	M A H L X
V O N	N B I M Y
W P O	O C J N Z
X Q P	P D K O A
Y R Q	Q E L P B
Z S R	R F M Q C
A T S	S G N R D
B U T	**T H O S E**
C V U	U I P T F
D W V	V J Q U G
E X W	W K R V H

*Page 42—*All Scripture is God-breathed and is useful for teaching, rebuking, correcting and training in righteousness. 2 Timothy 3:16

Prophecy never had its origin in the will of man, but men spoke from God as they were carried along by the Holy Spirit. 2 Peter 1:21

I have hidden Your Word in my heart that I might not sin against You. Psalm 119:11

A =		**M** =	
B =		**N** =	
C =		**O** =	
D =		**P** =	
E =		**R** =	
F =		**S** =	
G =		**T** =	
H =		**U** =	
I =		**V** =	
K =		**W** =	
L =		**Y** =	

L M N O P Q R S T U V W X Y Z A B C D E F G H I J K
A B C D E F G H I J K L M N O P Q R S T U V W X Y Z

But those who hope in the LORD will renew their strength. They will soar on wings like eagles; they will run and not grow weary, they will walk and not be faint. Isaiah 40:31

Page 44— In all your ways acknowledge Him, and He will make your paths straight. Proverbs 3:6

I will go before you and will level the mountains; I will break down gates of bronze and cut through bars of iron. Isaiah 45:2

I will instruct you and teach you in the way you should go; I will counsel you and watch over you. Psalm 32:8

Page 46— We speak of God's secret wisdom. 1 Corinthians 2:7

I will give you the treasures of darkness, riches stored in secret places. Isaiah 45:3

"The secret of the kingdom of God has been given to you." Mark 4:11

So then, men ought to regard us as servants of Christ and as those entrusted with the secret things of God. 1 Corinthians 4:1

Page 48— COMUNIATBDEFGHJKLPQRSVWXYZ
ABCDEFGHIJKLMNOPQRSTUVWXYZ

Call to Me and I will answer you and tell you great and unsearchable things you do not know. Jeremiah 33:3

Page 49— PRAYEBCDFGHIJKLMNOQSTUVWXZ
ABCDEFGHIJKLMNOPQRSTUVWXYZ

"If you believe, you will receive whatever you ask for in prayer." Matthew 21:22

Page 50— TALKOGDBCEFHIJMNPQRSUVWXYZ
ABCDEFGHIJKLMNOPQRSTUVWXYZ

"Ask and it will be given to you; seek and you will find; knock and the door will be opened to you." Matthew 7:7

Page 51— CLARITYBDEFGHJKMNOPQSUVWXZ
ABCDEFGHIJKLMNOPQRSTUVWXYZ

Before they call I will answer; while they are still speaking I will hear. Isaiah 65:24

Page 53—

1 2 3 4 5 6 7 8 9 1011 121314 15161718 1920212223242526 1 2 3
T I G U I K U Y M P Y L Z Q A P A V V B M X E M J D S P H
T H E R E F O R E G O A N D M A K E D I S C I P L E S O F

4 5 6 7 8 9 10 12 13 14 151617181920212223 242526 1 3 4 5 6 7
D P Q T H B R Y Y E, O O E J Z R B H B P E C L I O V K I
A L L N A T I O N S, B A P T I Z I N G T H E M I N T H E

8 9 10 12 1314 151617 181920212223 242526 1 2 3 4 5 6 7 8
S G T M X P E T R T P J Y W K U I Z L D S H F U R R
N A M E O F T H E F A T H E R A N D O F T H E S O N

91012 1314 151617 18192021 22232425261
F T K W O D S Q U C A O J H B L D P.
A N D O F T H E H O L Y S P I R I T. Matthew 28:19

Page 55—

1 2 3 4 5 6 7 8 9 10 11 12 1314151617 181920 212223242526 1 2 3
G P K Q X T G S T C R P I B F A T R F W J M A X A G T I G
"G O I N T O A L L T H E W O R L D A N D P R E A C H T H E

4 5 6 7 8 9 10 11 1213 141516 1718192021222324
J S T J U M F C E A N Z A S I W T N D K K.
G O O D N E W S T O A L L C R E A T I O N." Mark 16:15

1 2 3 4 5 6 7 8 9 10 11 12 13
L P X H I F I O W C R P D
"L O V E E A C H O T H E R." John 15:17